When Will

BLACK *Lives*

Matter?

Michael Parker

All rights reserved. No part of this publication may be reproduced, stored in a retrieval system, or transmitted in any way by any means electronic, mechanical, photocopy, recorded or otherwise without the prior permission of the copyright holder, except by reviewer who may quote brief passages in a review to be printed in magazine, newspaper or radio/TV announcement, as provided by USA copyright law. The author and the publisher will not be held responsible for errors within the manuscript.

Copyright 2025
ISBN 111111111111111

Printed in the USA

Dedication

To the families who have lost a loved one, my prayer is for strength for you and God's ever-loving hands to be upon you. May you have peace that passes all understanding (Philippians 4:7).

To those who marched, protested, prayed, and lifted their voices… Thank you.

To my Black communities, it is time to wake up and understand that Black lives will not matter until we change.

Introduction

The history of Black communities in America is marked by resilience and struggle. While external forces have played a significant role in shaping our experiences, we must also acknowledge the challenges we create for ourselves. It is time for us to come together, support each other, and work towards a better future for our children and grandchildren. Black lives will matter when we make the necessary changes within our communities.

I often wonder why we watch our families and communities decline, then wait until a national issue happens before we rise up in protest. We see Black folks get killed daily, yet we remain silent until the media shines a spotlight on the tragedy. This pattern of waiting for external validation before acting is detrimental to our progress. We must recognize that every life lost is a call to action, and we cannot afford to wait for others to acknowledge our pain. It is our responsibility to stand up, speak out, and work tirelessly to protect and uplift our communities.

This book is a call to action, a passionate plea for change. It is written to educate, inspire, and empower. We cannot afford to remain silent. Our future depends on the actions we take today!

Table of Contents

    Introduction

1. My Story — 1
2. The Build Up — 6
3. Personal Stories from Around the Country — 3
4. Well-Known Stories — 4
5. Current State as of 2020 — 27
6. Stopping Gun Violence And Black-on-Black Crimes — 35
7. Addressing Systemic Issues — 42
8. Empowering the Next Generation — 48
9. Successful Community Programs — 54
10. Conclusion — 59

1
My Story

I am a Black male who was once part of the problem. Growing up during the 1970s, 1980s, and 1990s in Detroit, I have been on the streets, done wrong in our community, and to our community. I was married at fifteen to a twenty-two-year-old woman for what I had, not because I was a man or so-called running things.

My journey began on the lower east side of Detroit, in the middle of Black Killers Grounds (French Road between Conner and Mack), where I

My Story

witnessed my first murder before the age of seven. By twelve, I was already involved in the drug trade.

Despite having a supportive family, my surroundings led me down a path of crime. I was arrested at thirteen and continued to hustle with the East Crew. I thought I would become a crime family boss, or at least that was my messed-up dream.

I sold weight starting with weed and then moved to cocaine, from the east side to the west side of Detroit, starting my freshman year of high school until the age of 21. I recall giving my wife cash to buy our first car when I was just 17 years old.

I don't want to go into detail regarding everything about that life, I'm just trying to give some background and context. I've seen a lot of things and done even more. That really needs to stay between me and God!

My Story

Fast forward 5 years…. Being at the wrong place, doing the wrong things began to change for me when I met two White doctors who believed in me and told me I was smart. My praying grandparents also played a significant role in my transformation. After being shot and stabbed, it took the death of my best friend to make me realize that enough was enough. Six months later, I began a journey of education and advocacy for those in need. I started coaching youth with the (PAL) Police Athletic League, and later, I began to mentor both youth and adults

As I continued my journey, I realized the importance of giving back to the community had shaped me. So, I started volunteering at local schools, sharing my story with students, and encouraging them to make positive choices. I also became involved in community organizations that focused on providing resources and support to at-risk youth. Through these efforts, I saw firsthand

My Story

the impact that mentorship and guidance could have on the lives of our youth.

One of the most rewarding experiences was coaching a youth football team. The kids on the team came from various backgrounds, but they all shared a common goal: to succeed both on and off the field. I emphasized the importance of discipline, teamwork, and perseverance, values which I had learned through my own struggles. Watching these young athletes grow and develop into confident, responsible individuals has been incredibly fulfilling.

While mentoring adults, I worked with individuals who were trying to turn their lives around, just as I had. We discussed their goals, challenges, and the steps they needed to take to achieve success. It was a humbling experience to see the positive changes in their lives and to know that I had played a part in their transformation.

My Story

My story is just one example of the resilience and strength that exists within Black communities. Despite the obstacles we face, we have the power to create positive change. By coming together, supporting each other, and working towards a common goal, we can build a brighter future for ourselves and future generations.

2
The Build Up

Slavery officially started in America around 1619 and continued for over 400 years. Between 1526 and 1867, over 12.5 million slaves were forcibly shipped to the United States from Africa, with only 10.7 million surviving the trip. Slavery was abolished in December 1865, freeing over 100,000 enslaved people. However, the legacy of slavery continues to impact Black communities today.

The Build Up

The Change

The year 1969 marked a significant turning point for Black culture in America. The founding of the Crips in Los Angeles and the subsequent formation of the Bloods in 1972 set the stage for decades of gang violence and rivalry. The rise of these gangs was fueled by socio-economic disparities, systemic racism, and a lack of opportunities for Black youth. The introduction of crack cocaine in the 1980s further exacerbated these issues, leading to a surge in addiction, crime, and violence within Black communities.

The war on drugs, initiated in the 1980s, disproportionately targeted Black individuals, resulting in mass incarceration and the destabilization of families and neighborhoods. This period saw an increase in police brutality and racial profiling, further straining the relationship between Black communities and law enforcement.

The Build Up

Despite these challenges, the resilience and determination of Black individuals and communities have led to considerable progress. The civil rights movement of the 1960s laid the foundation for ongoing efforts to achieve equality and justice. The Black Lives Matter movement, which gained momentum in the 2010s, has brought renewed attention to issues of police brutality, systemic racism, and social justice.

Chicago

In 1950, the Blackstone Rangers became Chicago's first gang. Chicago is considered the most gang-affiliated city in the United States, with a population ranging from 100,000 to 150,000 active gang members. Gang warfare and retaliation are common, with gangs responsible for 61% of homicides in Chicago in 2011. Homicides of Black

The Build Up

people increased significantly after the assassination of Martin Luther King Jr. in 1968.

Bronx

In the 1960s, the Black Spades emerged as a prominent street gang in the Bronx. Initially a teenage street organization, the Black Spades were influenced by the teachings of the Five-Percent Nation, Malcolm X, the Nation of Islam, and the Black Panthers. They organized to fight against racism and bigotry in their neighborhoods. Over time, the gang became more violent and lost focus of their original purpose.

Los Angeles

In 1969, the Crips were founded in Los Angeles. Initially an alliance between two autonomous gangs, the Crips became one of the largest and most violent street gangs in the United States. The gang's growth

The Build Up

and influence increased significantly in the early 1980s with the rise of crack cocaine. By the late 1980s, the Crips had become one of the nation's largest gangs.

In 1972, the Bloods were formed to compete against the Crips. The rivalry between the two gangs originated in the 1960s and led to widespread violence. The Bloods also became heavily involved in the distribution of crack cocaine, leading to a dramatic increase in membership.

Detroit

In the 1970s, Detroit saw the rise of several influential gangs that left a lasting mark on the city's history. Young Boys Incorporated (YBI) was one of the first major drug-dealing organizations, employing innovative distribution methods and recruiting teenagers to evade law enforcement. The A-Team, another notorious group, emerged around

The Build Up

the same time, known for its violent tactics and control over parts of the drug trade.

As the decades progressed, the Black Mafia Family (BMF) rose to prominence in the late 1990s and early 2000s, expanding from Detroit to become one of the largest drug trafficking and money laundering organizations in the country. While some of these groups initially formed under the guise of protecting their neighborhoods amidst racial unrest and injustice, they also contributed significantly to the violence, crime, and complex legacy of gang culture in Detroit.

Impact of Drugs

The introduction of crack cocaine in the 1980s had a devastating impact on Black communities across the United States. The drug epidemic led to a surge in addiction, crime, and violence. Families were torn apart, and entire neighborhoods were destabilized.

The Build Up

America's war on drugs, disproportionately targeted Black individuals and communities, which also resulted in the unjust wave of mass incarceration which further exacerbated the challenges faced by these communities.

Police Actions

The relationship between Black communities and White police officers has been fraught with tension and mistrust. Incidents of police brutality and racial profiling have led to widespread protests and calls for reform. The deaths of individuals such as George Floyd, Breonna Taylor, and many others have highlighted the systemic issues within law enforcement and the need for accountability and change.

The Build Up

Reflection on Black-on-Black Crime

The issue of Black-on-Black crime is a complex and multifaceted problem that requires a nuanced understanding. Black-on-Black crime is not a phenomenon that exists in isolation. It is deeply rooted in historical and socio-economic factors that have disproportionately affected Black communities for generations. The legacy of slavery, segregation, drugs, money, and keeping up with the Joneses has created conditions that contribute to an environment where crime can thrive.

By understanding the complex and interconnected factors that contribute to Black-on-Black crime, we can work towards creating solutions that address the root causes and promote a safer and more equitable society.

The Build Up

Powerful Quotes

You have seen how a man was made a slave, you shall see how a slave was made a man.

Frederick Douglass

The greatest tragedy is not the brutality of the evil people, but rather the silence of the good people.

Martin Luther King, Jr.

Black lives matter, and it is up to us to show that they matter not only in the face of police brutality but also within our own communities.

Unknown

Black-on-black crime is a symptom of a much larger problem. We need to address the systemic issues that contribute to violence and create opportunities for all.

Unknown

3

Personal Stories from Around the Country

Angela's Story

Angela grew up in the South Side of Chicago, a neighborhood often plagued by gang violence and economic hardship. She witnessed her brother being recruited into a gang at an early age, which deeply affected her. Despite these challenges, Angela focused on her education and became the first in her family to graduate from college. She now works as a community organizer, helping to provide resources and support for at-risk youth. Angela's dedication to

***Personal Stories
from Around the Country***

her community has inspired many young people to pursue their dreams and avoid the pitfalls of gang involvement.

Jamal's Story

Jamal was raised in the Bronx, surrounded by gang violence throughout his childhood. He lost several friends to gang-related incidents, which fueled his determination to make a difference. Jamal became a mentor for young boys in his neighborhood, teaching them the importance of education and staying away from gangs. His efforts have helped many young men find a sense of purpose and direction, steering them away from a life of crime.

Lisa's Story

Lisa grew up in Los Angeles during the height of the crack epidemic. She saw firsthand the devastating

***Personal Stories
from Around the Country***

effects of drug addiction on her community, including the loss of friends and family members. Determined to make a difference, Lisa became a social worker and now runs a rehabilitation center. She helps individuals recover from addiction and rebuild their lives, offering them hope and a chance for a better future.

Marcus's Story

Marcus was born and raised in Detroit, a city known for its high crime rates and economic challenges. He was involved in gang activities during his teenage years but turned his life around after being incarcerated. Marcus now works with former gang members, helping them reintegrate into society and find employment opportunities. His story of redemption and transformation serves as an inspiration to many who are looking to change their lives.

***Personal Stories
from Around the Country***

Charlie's Story

Charlie grew up in the Deep South, in a small town in Mississippi. He experienced the harsh realities of racial segregation and discrimination from a young age. Despite the odds, Charlie excelled in school and went on to attend college. He became a civil rights activist, working tirelessly to promote equality and justice for Black communities in the South. Charlie's efforts have led to significant changes in his town, including the desegregation of schools and the establishment of community programs to support Black youth. He organized peaceful protests, voter registration drives, and educational workshops to empower the community. Charlie's dedication to the cause has inspired many others to join the fight for civil rights and social justice.

*Personal Stories
from Around the Country*

Maria's Story

Maria grew up in the West Side of Atlanta, witnessing the impact of gang violence and drug addiction on her community. Determined to make a difference, Maria pursued a career in law enforcement. She now works as a police officer, advocating for community policing and building trust between law enforcement and the Black community. Maria's efforts have led to improved relations and reduced crime rates in her neighborhood. She has implemented various community outreach programs, such as youth mentorship initiatives and neighborhood watch groups, to foster collaboration and mutual respect. Maria also conducts workshops on conflict resolution and de-escalation techniques, aiming to bridge the gap between the police and the community they serve.

***Personal Stories
from Around the Country***

David's Story

David was raised in Baltimore, Maryland, a city with a long history of gang violence and drug addiction. Despite the obstacles, David focused on his education and became a teacher. He now works in a local school, mentoring young boys and girls and encouraging them to pursue their dreams. David's dedication to his students has made a significant impact on their lives and the community. He has established after-school programs that provide a safe space for students to engage in educational and recreational activities. David also organizes career workshops, inviting professionals from various fields to speak to the students and inspire them to explore different career paths. His mentorship has helped many students stay on the right track and avoid the pitfalls of gang involvement and drug addiction.

4

Well-Known Stories

The Story of Emmett Till

Emmett Till was a 14-year-old African American boy who was brutally murdered in Mississippi in 1955 for allegedly offending a White woman. His death and the subsequent acquittal of his killers sparked national outrage and became a catalyst for the Civil Rights Movement. Emmett's story is a stark reminder of the deep-seated racism and violence tthat Black communities have faced and continue to face.

Well-Known Stories

The Story of Rosa Parks

Rosa Parks is widely known as the "mother of the Civil Rights Movement." In 1955, she refused to give up her seat to a White passenger on a bus in Montgomery, Alabama. Her act of defiance led to the Montgomery Bus Boycott, a pivotal event in the fight for civil rights. Rosa Parks' courage and determination continue to inspire generations of activists. She was a personal family friend of my grandparents, uncles and aunties who I had the pleasure of meeting.

The Story of Martin Luther King, Jr.

Dr. Martin Luther King, Jr. was a prominent leader of the Civil Rights Movement. His advocacy for nonviolent resistance and his powerful speeches, including the famous "I Have a Dream" speech, played a crucial role in advancing civil rights in America. Dr. King's legacy of fighting for justice, equality, and peace continues to inspire people around the world.

The Story of Malcolm X

Malcolm X was a prominent figure in the Civil Rights Movement, known for his advocacy for Black empowerment and his critique of systemic racism. His journey from a troubled youth to a powerful leader and speaker is a testament to the transformative power of education and self-determination. Malcolm X's legacy continues to influence discussions on race, identity, and justice.

The Story of Harriet Tubman

Harriet Tubman was an abolitionist and political activist who escaped slavery and then made numerous missions to rescue enslaved people using the Underground Railroad. Her bravery and dedication to freedom have made her an enduring symbol of courage and resistance against oppression.

The Story of Frederick Douglass

Frederick Douglass was a former enslaved person who became a leading abolitionist, writer, and orator. His powerful speeches and writings, including his autobiography, "Narrative of the Life of Frederick Douglass, an American Slave," highlighted the horrors of slavery and advocated for the rights of African Americans. Douglass' legacy continues to inspire the fight for justice and equality.

These stories, both those from current as well as well-known individuals, highlight the resilience, strength, and determination of individuals who have worked to overcome adversity and create positive changes in their communities. By sharing these narratives, we can inspire others to join the fight for

Well-Known Stories

justice and equality and work towards a brighter future for all.

5

Current State as of 2020

Since 2020, the Black community in America has experienced both progress and ongoing challenges. The heightened awareness and activism following the tragic death of George Floyd and the subsequent global Black Lives Matter protests have led to some significant changes, but there is still much work to be done.

Racial Justice and Police Reform: The murder of George Floyd in 2020 sparked a national and global outcry against police brutality and systemic

Current State as of 2020

racism. This led to increased scrutiny of police practices and calls for reform. Some cities and states have implemented changes, such as banning chokeholds, requiring body cameras, and increasing accountability for police misconduct. However, progress has been uneven, and many activists feel that the momentum for change has slowed. According to a 2025 Pew Research Center study, 72% of U.S. adults believe that the focus on racial inequality has not led to significant changes that have helped the Black community.

Economic Disparities: The economic impact of the COVID-19 pandemic disproportionately affected Black communities, exacerbating existing disparities. While there have been efforts to support Black-owned businesses and increase economic opportunities, challenges remain. The unemployment rate for Black Americans was 6.3% in 2023, compared to 3.8% for the overall

Current State as of 2020

population. Additionally, many of the financial commitments made by corporations and philanthropists in 2020 were short-term and have not resulted in sustained support for Black communities.

Healthcare Access: Health disparities continue to affect Black communities, with higher rates of chronic diseases such as hypertension and diabetes. The COVID-19 pandemic highlighted these disparities, as Black Americans experienced higher rates of infection and mortality. Efforts to improve healthcare access and address these disparities are ongoing, but significant gaps remain. In 2023, 92.0% of people in the United States had health insurance, but the uninsured rate for children under the age of 19 increased by 0.5 percentage points to 5.8% between 2022 and 2023.

Educational Opportunities: Educational disparities persist, with Black students more likely to

Current State as of 2020

attend high-poverty schools and receive less funding compared to their white counterparts. The graduation rate for Black students is 81%, compared to 90% for White students. Efforts to address these disparities include advocating for equitable funding and providing scholarships, mentorship, and resources for students.

Mental Health: Mental health disparities also continue to affect Black communities. According to the KFF Survey of Racism, Discrimination, and Health, 39% of Black adults reported receiving mental health services in the past three years, compared to 50% of White adults. Additionally, 46% of Black adults reported difficulty finding a provider who could understand their background and experiences. There is a growing recognition of the need for culturally sensitive mental health services and increased funding for mental health programs.

Current State as of 2020

Civic Engagement: The Black community has shown increased civic engagement, with higher voter turnout and participation in local government and advocacy efforts. In the 2020 U.S. presidential election, Black voter turnout was 62%. This engagement is crucial for creating positive change and ensuring that the voices of Black Americans are heard in the decision-making process.

Community Initiatives: Various community initiatives have emerged to address these challenges and support the Black community. Programs such as the Harlem Children's Zone, My Brother's Keeper, and Black Girls Code provide comprehensive support, mentorship, and opportunities for young people. These initiatives aim to break the cycle of poverty, promote education, and empower the next generation.

Current State as of 2020

Unemployment Rates: The unemployment rate for Black Americans was 6.3% in 2023, compared to 3.8% for the overall population.

Financial Commitments: Many of the financial commitments made by corporations and philanthropists in 2020 were short-term and have not resulted in sustained support for Black communities.

Income Inequality: Over the past 50 years, the highest-earning 20% of U.S. households have steadily brought in a larger share of the country's total income. In 2018, households in the top fifth of earners (with incomes of $130,001 or more that year) brought in 52% of all U.S. income, more than the lower four-fifths combined.

Gini Coefficient: Income inequality in the U.S. is the highest of all the G7 nations, with a Gini coefficient of 0.434 in 2017. In comparison, the

Current State as of 2020

Gini coefficient ranged from 0.326 in France to 0.392 in the UK.

Black-White Income Gap: The difference in median household incomes between white and Black Americans has grown from about $23,800 in 1970 to $33,000 in 2018 (as measured in 2018 dollars). Median Black household income was 61% of median white household income in 2018, up modestly from 56% in 1970.

Economic Inequality Perception: Overall, 61% of Americans say there is too much economic inequality in the country today. Among Republicans and those who lean toward the GOP, 41% say there is too much inequality in the U.S., compared with 78% of Democrats and Democratic leaders.

While progress has been made since 2020, the Black community continues to face significant challenges. It is essential to sustain the momentum for change and continue advocating for policies and

Current State as of 2020

initiatives that promote equity and justice. By coming together and supporting one another, we can work towards a brighter future for the Black community.

Powerful Quotes:

For to be free is not merely to cast off one's chains, but to live in a way that respects and enhances the freedom of others.
Nelson Mandela:

The need for change bulldozed a road down the center of my mind.
Maya Angelou:

Not everything that is faced can be changed, but nothing can be changed until it is faced.
James Baldwin:

6

Stopping Gun Violence and Black-on-Black Crimes

Gun violence and Black-on-Black crimes are pressing issues that continue to plague our communities. These problems are not only a matter of public safety but also deeply rooted in historical, socio-economic, and systemic factors. It is time for us to come together, take decisive action, and work towards creating safer and more equitable communities. Here is a comprehensive call to action to address these critical issues:

*Stopping Gun Violence
and Black-on-Black Crimes*

Personal Responsibility and Collective Action

While systemic change is essential, we must also recognize the role of personal responsibility in addressing violence within our communities. Each of us has a part to play in creating a safer environment. This includes being a positive role model, speaking out against violence, and supporting those who are working to make a difference. By taking collective action, we can create a culture of accountability and support that empowers individuals to make positive choices.

Stopping gun violence and Black-on-Black crimes requires a multifaceted approach that addresses the root causes, empowers individuals, and promotes systemic change. It is a call to action for all of us to come together, support each other, and work towards creating safer and more equitable communities. By understanding the complexities of these issues and taking decisive action, we can build a brighter future for ourselves and future generations.

Building Strong Communities

Communities play a pivotal role in shaping the lives of their members. By coming together, we can create environments that foster growth, support, and unity. Here are some ways we can strengthen our communities:

<u>Support Local Businesses:</u> Patronizing Black-owned businesses is essential for building economic stability within the community. According to the U.S. Census Bureau, there are over 2.6 million Black-owned businesses in the United States, contributing approximately $150 billion to the economy annually. By supporting these businesses, we not only help them thrive but also encourage entrepreneurship. Providing resources

and mentorship for aspiring business owners can further stimulate economic growth and create job opportunities.

Create Safe Spaces: Establishing community centers and safe spaces is crucial for fostering a sense of belonging and support. These spaces can serve as hubs for educational programs, recreational activities, and mental health resources. By offering a variety of services, we can ensure that individuals have access to the support they need to thrive.

Promote Civic Engagement: Encouraging community members to participate in local government, vote in elections, and advocate for policies that benefit the community is vital for creating positive change. Civic engagement empowers individuals to have a voice in the decisions that affect their lives and helps to build a more inclusive and responsive government. The

***Stopping Gun Violence
and Black-on-Black Crimes***

figures mentioned—such as Black voter turnout in the 2020 U.S. presidential election (62%) and civic engagement rates from 2023—originate from surveys and reports by the U.S. Census Bureau. Voter turnout data comes from post-election reports like "Voting and Registration in the Election of November 2020." The statistics on civic engagement are gathered through the Civic Engagement and Volunteering Supplement, part of the Census Bureau's Current Population Survey (CPS). Research organizations like the National Conference on Citizenship also analyze and report on this data.

Organize Community Events: Hosting events that celebrate Black culture, history, and achievements can foster a sense of pride and unity within the community. These events provide opportunities for individuals to connect, learn, and celebrate together. By highlighting the rich cultural

***Stopping Gun Violence
and Black-on-Black Crimes***

heritage and accomplishments of the community, we can inspire future generations and strengthen communal bonds.

Powerful Quotes

> *Never doubt that a small group of thoughtful, committed citizens can change the world; indeed, it's the only thing that ever has.*
>
> **Margaret Mead**

> *I alone cannot change the world, but I can cast a stone across the waters to create many ripples.*
>
> **Mother Teresa:**

> *In every community, there is work to be done. In every nation, there are wounds to heal. In every heart, there is the power to do it.*
>
> **Marianne Williamson**

Stopping Gun Violence and Black-on-Black Crimes

There is no power for change greater than a community discovering what it cares about.

Margaret J. Wheatley

7

Addressing Systemic Issues

To create lasting change, we must address systemic issues that impact Black communities. Here are some ways we can work towards this goal:

Advocate for Criminal Justice Reform: Support initiatives that aim to reform the criminal justice system, reduce mass incarceration, and address police brutality.

Addressing Systemic Issues

Advocate for policies that promote fairness and accountability. According to the Sentencing Project, Black Americans are incarcerated at more than five times the rate of White Americans. By pushing for reforms such as eliminating mandatory minimum sentences and promoting restorative justice practices, we can work towards a more equitable system

Improve Access to Healthcare: Work to ensure that Black communities have access to quality healthcare services. Address health disparities and promote preventive care and wellness programs. The Centers for Disease Control and Prevention (CDC) reports that Black Americans have higher rates of chronic diseases such as hypertension and diabetes compared to other racial groups. In 2023, 92.0% of people in the United States had health insurance, either for some or all of the year. However, the uninsured rate for children under the

Addressing Systemic Issues

age of 19 increased by 0.5 percentage points to 5.8% between 2022 and 2023. By advocating for increased funding for community health centers and expanding Medicaid, we can help bridge the gap in healthcare access.

Enhance Educational Opportunities: Advocate for equitable funding for schools in Black communities. Support programs that provide scholarships, mentorship, and resources for students. The National Center for Education Statistics (NCES) found that schools in predominantly Black neighborhoods receive significantly less funding than those in predominantly White neighborhoods. According to the 2023 Report on the Condition of Education, Black students are more likely to attend high-poverty schools, with 45% of Black students attending such schools compared to 8% of White students. Additionally, the graduation rate for Black

Addressing Systemic Issues

students is 81%, compared to 90% for White students. By pushing for policies that ensure fair distribution of educational resources, we can help create a level playing field for all students.

Combat Racial Discrimination: Stand against racial discrimination in all its forms. Promote diversity and inclusion in workplaces, schools, and public spaces. The Equal Employment Opportunity Commission (EEOC) reports that Black workers are more likely to experience discrimination in hiring, promotions, and pay compared to their white counterparts. By advocating for stronger anti-discrimination laws and promoting diversity training programs, we can work towards a more inclusive society.

Address Mental Health Disparities: Work to ensure that Black communities have access to quality mental health services. Address mental health disparities and promote mental wellness

Addressing Systemic Issues

programs. According to the KFF Survey of Racism, Discrimination, and Health, 39% of Black adults reported receiving mental health services in the past three years, compared to 50% of White adults. Additionally, 46% of Black adults reported difficulty finding a provider who could understand their background and experiences. By advocating for culturally sensitive mental health services and increasing funding for mental health programs, we can help bridge the gap in mental health care access.

Improve Employment Rates: Advocate for policies that promote job creation and economic stability within Black communities. According to the U.S. Bureau of Labor Statistics, the national unemployment rate remained below 4% throughout 2023, with the labor force participation rate at 62.6% in the fourth quarter. However, Black Americans continue to face higher unemployment rates compared to their white counterparts. In 2023,

Addressing Systemic Issues

the unemployment rate for Black Americans was 6.3%, compared to 3.8% for the overall population. By supporting initiatives that provide job training, career development, and entrepreneurship opportunities, we can work towards reducing employment disparities and promoting economic growth.

Powerful Quote:

It's up to all of us—Black, White, everyone—no matter how well-meaning we think we might be, to do the honest, uncomfortable work of rooting it out.
Michelle Obama

8

Empowering the Next Generation

The future of the Black community hinges on our ability to empower the next generation. By investing in youth, we can cultivate a brighter and more equitable future. Here are some ways we can achieve this:

Mentoring Our Youth: Providing mentorship and guidance to young people is crucial. Mentors can help young people set ambitious yet achievable goals, develop essential life skills, and navigate the

Empowering the Next Generation

myriad challenges they may face. By offering consistent support and encouragement, mentors can play a transformative role in the lives of young individuals, helping them to realize their full potential.

Encourage Leadership: Inspiring young people to take on leadership roles within their schools, communities, and beyond is vital for fostering a sense of responsibility and empowerment. By providing opportunities for youth to develop leadership skills, such as through student government, community service projects, or youth-led initiatives, we can nurture the next generation of leaders who will advocate for positive change and drive progress within their communities.

Promote Financial Literacy: Teaching financial literacy to young people is essential for building economic stability and independence. Financial education should cover topics such as budgeting,

Empowering the Next Generation

saving, investing, and understanding credit. By equipping youth with the knowledge and skills to manage their finances effectively, we can empower them to make informed decisions that will benefit them throughout their lives.

Support Creative Expression: Encouraging young people to express themselves through art, music, writing, and other creative outlets is a powerful tool for empowerment and healing. Creative expression allows youth to explore their identities, process their emotions, and communicate their experiences in meaningful ways. By providing access to arts programs, workshops, and platforms for highlighting their talents, we can help young people find their voices and build confidence in their abilities.

Foster a Sense of Community: Building a strong sense of community is essential for the well-being and development of young people. By creating safe

Empowering the Next Generation

and supportive environments where youth feel valued and connected, we can help them develop a sense of belonging and purpose. Community centers, after-school programs, and youth organizations can provide spaces for young people to come together, build relationships, and engage in positive activities.

Address Systemic Barriers: It is important to recognize and address the systemic barriers that disproportionately affect Black youth. This includes advocating for equitable access to quality education, healthcare, and economic opportunities. By working to dismantle these barriers, we can create a more just and inclusive society where all young people can thrive.

Promote Mental Health and Well-being: Supporting the mental health and well-being of young people is crucial for their overall development. Providing access to mental health

Empowering the Next Generation

resources, counseling, and wellness programs can help youth navigate the challenges they face and build resilience. It is also important to create environments where mental health is openly discussed and designated, allowing young people to seek help without fear of judgment.

By focusing on these areas, we can empower the next generation to lead fulfilling and impactful lives. Investing in the youth is not only an investment in their future but also in the future of our communities as a whole. Together, we can create a brighter and more equitable future for all.

Powerful Quotes:

In every community, there is work to be done. In every nation, there are wounds to heal. In every heart, there is the power to do it.

Marianne Williamson

Empowering the Next Generation

There is no power for change greater than a community discovering what it cares about.

Margaret J. Wheatley

There is nothing I'm any more passionate about than empowering the next generation.

T. D. Jakes

9
Successful Community Programs

The stories of individuals like Angela, Jamal, Lisa, Marcus, Charlie, Maria, and David highlight the diverse ways in which Black people have worked to overcome adversity and create positive change in their communities. From community organizing and mentorship to law enforcement and civil rights activism, these individuals exemplify the strength and resilience of Black culture.

Successful Community Programs

Here are some examples of successful community programs that have made a positive impact:

Harlem Children's Zone

The Harlem Children's Zone is a nonprofit organization that provides comprehensive support to children and families in Harlem, New York. The program offers educational, social, and health services, including early childhood education, after-school programs, college preparation, and family support services. The goal is to break the cycle of poverty and help children achieve academic and personal success.

My Brother's Keeper

My Brother's Keeper is an initiative launched by President Barack Obama to address opportunity gaps faced by young men of color. The program focuses on mentoring, education, and employment opportunities. It aims to ensure that all young

Successful Community Programs

people can reach their full potential, regardless of their background.

Black Girls Code

Black Girls Code is a nonprofit organization that empowers young Black girls to pursue careers in technology and computer science. The program offers workshops, coding classes, and mentorship opportunities to help girls develop technical skills and confidence. The goal is to increase diversity in the tech industry and provide opportunities for underrepresented groups.

The Brotherhood/Sister Sol

The Brotherhood/Sister Sol is a youth development organization based in Harlem, New York. The program provides comprehensive support to young people, including education, leadership training, and social justice advocacy. The goal is to empower youth to become leaders and change-makers in their communities.

The Dream Defenders

The Dream Defenders is a social justice organization that advocates for the rights of marginalized communities. The program focuses on issues such as criminal justice reform, education, and economic justice. The goal is to create a more equitable society and empower individuals to fight for their rights.

Exploring initiatives and resources at the local, regional, and national levels is vital for identifying programs that align with your community's needs and aspirations. Whether through nonprofit organizations dedicated to

Successful
Community Programs

education, social justice, or technology, or grassroots movements aiming to address systemic inequities, there are countless opportunities available to foster empowerment and growth. Conducting thorough research and engaging in dialogue with community leaders can uncover programs tailored to address specific challenges while promoting unity and advancement. By actively seeking out these initiatives, individuals and families can contribute to the collective effort of building a stronger, more resilient community.

10

Conclusion

The history of Black communities in America includes both resilience and hardship. External factors have significantly influenced these experiences, but internal challenges also exist. Continued efforts within Black communities aim to foster mutual support and work towards positive outcomes for future generations. The significance of Black lives is linked to ongoing changes and developments within these communities.

Conclusion

Strengthening Family Bonds

Strong families are the foundation of thriving communities. As families, we can:

Prioritize Education: Encourage children to excel in school and pursue higher education. Create a home environment that values learning and provides the necessary support for academic success.

Foster Open Communication: Maintain open and honest communication within the family. Discuss challenges, aspirations, and the importance of unity and support.

Promote Positive Role Models: Highlight the achievements of successful Black individuals in various fields. Encourage children to look up to these role models and aspire to make a positive impact.

Conclusion

Engage in Family Activities: Spend quality time together through activities that strengthen family bonds, such as family dinners, game nights, and community service projects.

Building Strong Communities

Communities play a crucial role in shaping the lives of their members. As communities, we can:

Support Local Businesses: Patronize Black-owned businesses to help build economic stability within the community. Encourage entrepreneurship and provide resources for aspiring business owners.

Create Safe Spaces: Establish community centers and safe spaces where individuals can gather, learn, and support one another. These spaces can offer educational programs, recreational activities, and mental health resources.

Conclusion

Promote Civic Engagement: Encourage community members to participate in local government, vote in elections, and advocate for policies that benefit the community. Civic engagement is essential for creating positive change.

Organize Community Events: Host events that celebrate Black culture, history, and achievements. These events can foster a sense of pride and unity within the community.

Addressing Systemic Issues

To create lasting change, we must address systemic issues that impact Black communities. We can:

Advocate for Criminal Justice Reform: Support initiatives that aim to reform the criminal justice system, reduce mass incarceration, and address police brutality. Advocate for policies that promote fairness and accountability.

Conclusion

Improve Access to Healthcare: Work to ensure that Black communities have access to quality healthcare services. Address health disparities and promote preventive care and wellness programs.

Enhance Educational Opportunities: Advocate for equitable funding for schools in Black communities. Support programs that provide scholarships, mentorship, and resources for students.

Combat Racial Discrimination: Stand against racial discrimination in all its forms. Promote diversity and inclusion in workplaces, schools, and public spaces.

Empowering the Next Generation

The future of Black communities depends on empowering the next generation. We can:

Conclusion

Mentor Youth: Provide mentorship and guidance to young people. Help them set goals, develop skills, and navigate challenges.

Encourage Leadership: Inspire young people to take on leadership roles within their schools, communities, and beyond. Provide opportunities for them to develop leadership skills.

Promote Financial Literacy: Teach financial literacy to young people, including budgeting, saving, and investing. Financial knowledge is essential for building economic stability.

Support Creative Expression: Encourage young people to express themselves through art, music, writing, and other creative outlets. Creative expression can be a powerful tool for empowerment and healing.

Conclusion

By taking these steps as families and communities, we can repair and build up Black lives mattering. Together, we can create a future where Black lives are valued, respected, and empowered.

I leave you with this - "Carry each other's burdens, and in this way, you will fulfill the law of Christ." (Galatians 6:2)

Your journey towards understanding and making a difference starts here.

References

These references are cited throughout your book to support various points and provide credible sources. I encourage you to dive deeper into these materials and expand your knowledge. Take the time to educate yourself on these important topics and become an advocate for change.

Views of Race, Policing and Black Lives Matter in the 5 Years Since George Floyd's Killing. (May 7, 2025) Pew Research Center from 2025.
https://www.pewresearch.org/race-and-ethnicity/2025/05/07/views-of-race-policing-and-black-lives-matter-in-the-5-years-since-george-floyds-killing/

Civilian unemployment rate, U.S. Bureau of Statistics (2023), Published (September 10, 2024),
https://www.bls.gov/charts/employment-situation/civilian-unemployment-rate.htm

High School Graduation Rates, National Center for Education Statistics (NCES), (May 2024), https://nces.ed.gov/programs/coe/indicator/coi/high-school-graduation-rates

Civil Rights Data Collection, Department of Education, (2020 – 2021), https://civilrightsdata.ed.gov/profile/us?surveyYear=2020

Racism, Discrimination, and Health (June 6- August 14, 2023), KFF Survey, Retrieved January 15, 2025 from, https://www.kff.org/racial-equity-and-health-policy/issue-brief/racial-and-ethnic-disparities-in-mental-health-care-findings-from-the-kff-survey-of-racism-discrimination-and-health/

Racial/Ethnic Disparities in Pregnancy-Related Deaths — United States, 2007–2016, Centers for Disease Control and Prevention (CDC), (September 6, 2019, https://www.cdc.gov/mmwr/volumes/68/wr/mm6835a3.htm

Voter turnout rates among black voters in U.S. presidential elections from 1964 to 2020, O'Neil A., (July 4, 2024) https://www.statista.com/statistics/1096577/voter-turnout-black-voters-presidential-elections-historical

Black Turnout in the 2020 Election, Newport F., (September 25, 2020), GALLUP, https://news.gallup.com/opinion/polling-matters/320903/black-turnout-2020-election.aspx

Unemployment rates remained low through the third quarter of 2023 though labor market disparities persist, Moore K., Economic Policy Institute, (2023 Q3), https://www.epi.org/indicators/state-unemployment-race-ethnicity-2023-q3/

6 facts about economic inequality in the U.S., Pew Research Center, (February 7, 2020), https://www.pewresearch.org/short-reads/2020/02/07/6-facts-about-economic-inequality-in-the-u-s/

Income Inequality by Country 2025, World Population Review, (2022), Retrieved July, 2025 https://worldpopulationreview.com/country-rankings/income-inequality-by-country

6 facts about economic inequality in the U.S., Pew Research Center, (February 7, 2020), https://www.pewresearch.org/short-reads/2020/02/07/6-facts-about-economic-inequality-in-the-u-s/

Why Supporting Black Owned Businesses Build Wealth, Opportunity, and Stronger Communities,

Black Business Lists, (April 26, 2025), https://blackbusinesslists.com/support-black-owned-businesses/ and

Black Ownership Statistics 2024https://advocacy.sba.gov/2024/02/01/facts-about-small-business-black-ownership-statistics-2024/ and Annual Business Survey Release Provides Data on Minority-Owned, Veteran-Owned and Women-Owned Businesses, U.S. Census Bureau , (January 28, 2021), https://www.census.gov/newsroom/press-releases/2021/annual-business-survey.html

www.ingramcontent.com/pod-product-compliance
Lightning Source LLC
Chambersburg PA
CBHW060657030426
42337CB00017B/2664